MEDIEVAL REALMS

stick a picture here

Name ______________________ **Class** ______________________

Year ______________________ **School** ______________________

Timeline of the Middle Ages

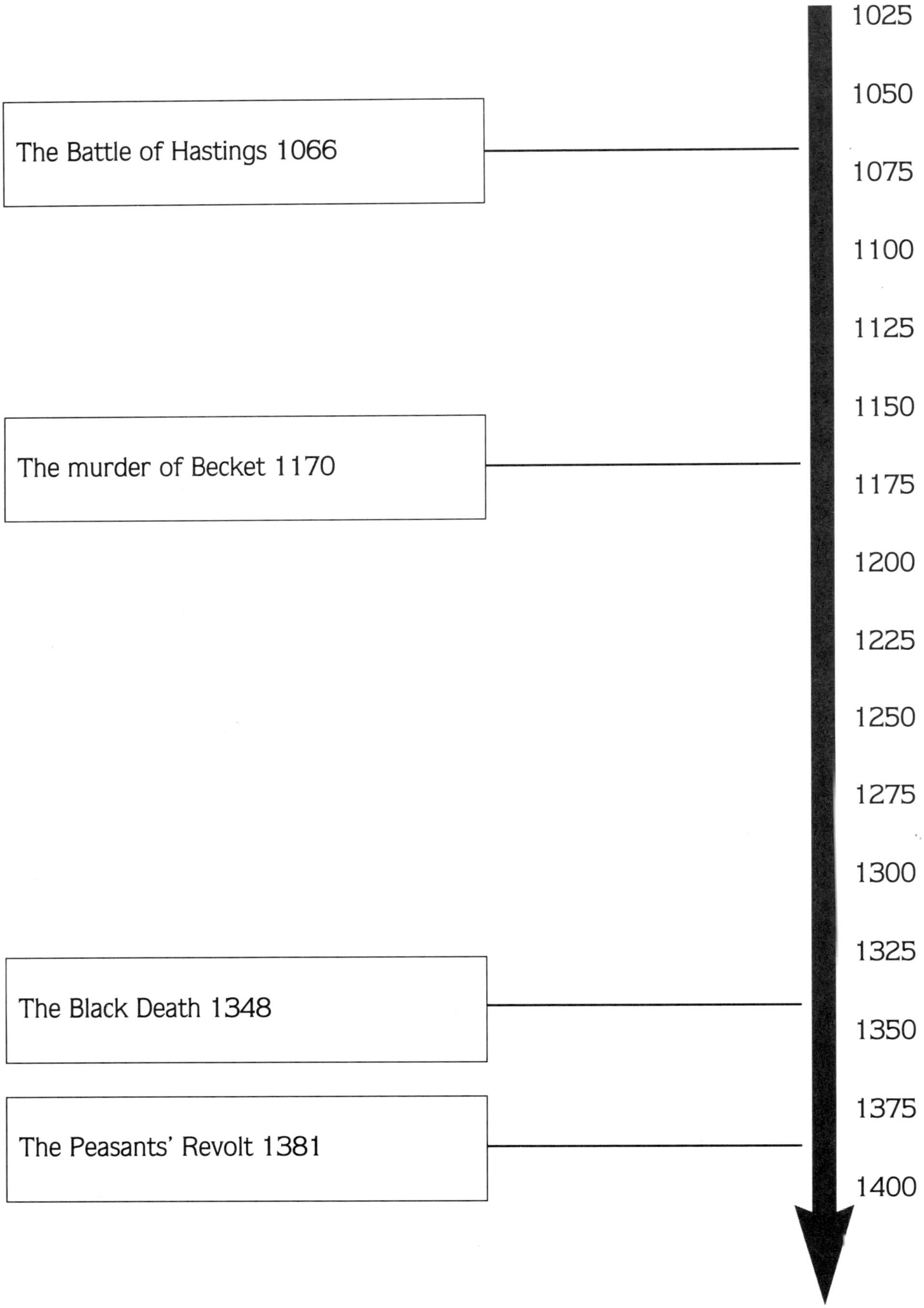

S·H·P
THE SCHOOLS HISTORY PROJECT

DISCOVERING THE PAST

MEDIEVAL REALMS

PICTURE PACK WORKBOOK

COLIN SHEPHARD ANN MOORE

Contrasts and Connections Pupils' Book ISBN 0-7195-4938-8
Teachers' Resource Book ISBN 0-7195-4962-0
Discovering Medieval Realms Pupils' Book ISBN 0-7195-5177-3
Teachers' Evaluation Pack ISBN 0-7195-5178-1
Medieval Realms Special Needs Support Materials
Picture Pack ISBN 0-7195-5382-2
Teachers' Resource Book ISBN 0-7195-5381-4

First published 1995
by John Murray (Publishers) Ltd
50 Albemarle Street
London W1X 4BD

Reprinted in 1995

Illustrations by Peter Bull Art Studio, Ann Moore, John Townson/Creation

Printed and bound in Great Britain by St Edmundsbury Press Ltd,
Bury St Edmunds, Suffolk

A CIP catalogue record for this book is available from the British Library

ISBN 0-7195-7056-5
ISBN 0-7195-7057-3 Pack of 5 workbooks

Contents

Date completed

The Battle of Hastings in 1066

1. King Harold is crowned ....
2. Is it in the tapestry? ....
3. The Battle of Hastings ....
4. The Bayeux Tapestry as a source of evidence ....

What was life like in the Middle Ages?

5. Finding out about a medieval village ....
6. Ploughing ....
7. Materials which were used in the Middle Ages ....
8. Spotting anachronisms ....
9. A man and a woman in the field ....
10. Peasants working in the field ....
11. The incomplete harvest ....
12. The peasants' year ....
13. The harvest wagon ....
14. Carrying a sack of corn ....
15. The water mill with eel nets ....
16. Where will you put your mill? ....
17. Sheep in a sheepfold ....
18. 'Sheepish connections' ....
19. The blacksmith's shop ....
20. A medieval village scene ....
21. Preparing for a feast ....
22. The feast ....
23. The kitchen in the manor house ....
24. The medieval village: piecing the evidence together ....
25. The town market place ....
26. Heaven and hell ....
27. Noah's Ark ....
28. The Black Death ....

Problems facing medieval kings

29. The murder of Thomas Becket ....
30. The Peasants' Revolt ....

1

Picture Pack

King Harold is crowned

This drawing is a copy of Picture Source 1.

Your task

1. Colour in the man in this picture who you think is King Harold.

2. How do we know he is a king?

3. Colour in the man who you think is Archbishop Stigant in this picture.

4. How do we know he is an archbishop?

2

Picture Pack

Is it in the tapestry?

Picture Sources 1–5 all come from the Bayeux Tapestry. This is a long piece of cloth with pictures sewn all the way along it. Get to know the tapestry by searching for various things in it.

Your task

Look at Picture Sources 1–5 and put a circle round any of the objects below which you can find in them.

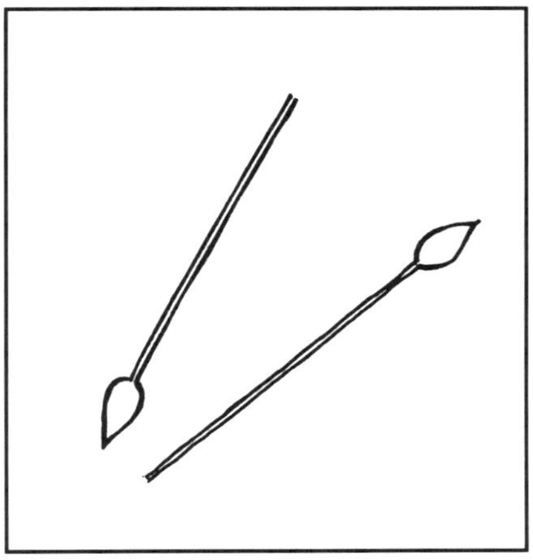

3

Picture Pack

There are three pages to this task

The Battle of Hastings

Picture Sources 1–5 come from the Bayeux Tapestry.

The pictures tell the story of three men. All three were kings of England in a single year, 1066. The first king was Edward, the second was Harold, and the third was William.

The story begins with King Edward sending his friend Harold to Normandy in France to meet Duke William. King Edward wants William to become king when he dies.

Harold spends a long time in France getting to know Duke William. He helps William to beat some of his enemies in France. Harold swears to obey William.

However, when King Edward dies, Harold decides to make himself King of England.

Picture Sources 1–5 tell the rest of the story.

Your task

1. Copy out each of these captions on to a separate piece of paper:

The Normans met the English at Hastings. The two armies fought hard.	Duke William and his army sailed from Normandy to England.
After King Edward died, Harold was crowned King of England.	King Harold was killed. The Normans had won.
Duke William of Normandy was angry that Harold had become king. He began to gather weapons and armour for his army.	

2. Match the captions to Picture Sources 1–5.
3. Now put the captions and pictures into order.

3

page 2

The Norman army gets ready

The Norman army needed lots of armour and weapons.

Your task

The picture below is an outline of Picture Source 2. Match the numbers on the picture with these descriptions:

Description	Number
■ daggers for when the English soldiers are close	
■ arrows to shoot at the English	
■ a coat of armour to protect a Norman soldier against English arrows and swords	
■ helmets to protect the soldiers' heads	
■ a sword for sword fighting	
■ an axe (Do you think this would be used in the fighting?)	

3

page 3

The Battle

Picture Source 4 shows one moment in the middle of the Battle of Hastings.

Your task 1

1. Describe what the men are wearing.

2. Explain what you think is happening in the picture.

Your task 2

Write a paragraph explaining the story of the Battle of Hastings in your own words. Make sure that in your story you describe what you can see happening in Picture Sources 1–5.

4

Picture Pack

The Bayeux Tapestry as a source of evidence

The Bayeux Tapestry is very useful as evidence about medieval life. For example, it gives us information about:

- the weapons which soldiers used
- the hairstyles people had
- the ships which were used to carry armies.

Your task

1. Examine Picture Sources 1–5. Write down at least one thing the tapestry tells us about each of the following:
   - The soldiers' weapons ______
   - The people's hairstyles ______
   - The ships in which the soldiers sailed ______

2. Make a list below of other things which the Bayeux Tapestry gives us evidence about.

5

Picture Pack

There are three pages to this task

Finding out about a medieval village

In the Middle Ages most people lived in villages. A good way of finding out about these villages is to look at pictures painted by people who were alive at that time. They often painted ordinary people doing ordinary things, such as in Picture Sources 6–15.

Look at one of these pictures together in a small group and see how much you can find out about medieval life.

Asking the questions

The first step is to make your own list of questions about what is going on in the picture.

For example:

- If you have Picture Source 13, you might want to ask: Why do the women look sad?
- If you have Picture Source 7, you might like to ask: What is the man wearing around his waist?
- If you have Picture Source 12, you might want to ask: What are those black lines in the water?

Your task

1. Choose a picture source for your group and discuss what you would like to find out about it.
2. Now write your questions about this picture source here:

Picture Source number _____

Things we would like to find out about this Picture Source

1. ______________________________

2. ______________________________

3. ______________________________

4. ______________________________

5. ______________________________

Finding the answers

You are now going to try to write your own answers to some of the questions you asked on the first page. For example, if you were answering the example questions on the last page you might write:

The women look sad because they have to work so hard.
The man is wearing a belt with some gloves tucked in it.
We think that the black lines are old-fashioned fishing nets.

Your task

1. Look at your list of questions, and as a group try to find an answer to as many of them as you can.
   - You could look things up in books.
   - You could make guesses from things you already know.
   - You could make guesses from what you see in the picture.

2. Write your answers here:

Picture Source number _____

1. ______________________________
   ____
2. ______________________________
   ____
3. ______________________________
   ____
4. ______________________________
   ____
5. ______________________________
   ____

3. When you have finished your answers, as a group choose one of your questions and copy it out with its answer on to a separate sheet of paper.

Recording your discoveries

When the whole class has finished asking their questions and finding out the answers, your teacher will display the picture sources on the wall. Underneath them will be all your questions and answers.

This display is your evidence about life in a medieval village.

Your task

1. On your own, look carefully at the evidence displayed on the wall.
2. Choose four things you have discovered about medieval villages that you did not know before. Write them down in the box below.

The four things that I have found out about life in a medieval village are:

1. ______________________________

____

2. ______________________________

____

3. ______________________________

____

4. ______________________________

____

I therefore conclude that this has helped me to understand a little bit about life in medieval villages.

Signed ______________________________ *(historical researcher)*

6
Picture Pack

Ploughing

Your task

1. Look at Picture Source 6 and describe what is happening in it.
   - The man on the left is
   - The man in the middle is
   - The plough is being pulled by
2. Do you think everyone in the village would have owned a plough and some oxen?
3. Explain your answer carefully.

If you were in charge of the farming equipment in a medieval village, how many ploughs and how many oxen would you have?

7

Picture Pack

Materials which were used in the Middle Ages

Your task

1. Look at Picture Source 7. What do you think is happening?

2. What time of year do you think it is?

3. Which items of clothing that the man is wearing are made out of leather?

4. Which items of clothing that the man is wearing are made out of wool?

5. What do you think the seed box is made out of?

6. Make a list of all the materials you can think of that would not have existed in the Middle Ages (for example, nylon).

8

Picture Pack

Spotting anachronisms

'Anachronism' is a word used to describe something that has been put into the wrong period of time. For example, it would be an anachronism if a picture showed an aeroplane dropping bombs on William the Conqueror at the Battle of Hastings, because aeroplanes did not exist until almost nine hundred years after the Battle of Hastings.

Your task

1. Look carefully at this picture of a man in the Middle Ages sowing seed. Put a circle round each anachronism – that is, anything that would not have existed in the Middle Ages.
2. Add some more anachronisms to the picture.

9

Picture Pack

A man and a woman in the field

Picture Source 8 shows a man and a woman working in a field.

Your task

1. Look carefully at Picture Source 8. What do you think the man and woman are doing?

2. Why do you think the man is wearing gloves?

3. What tools are they using?

4. How do you think the man and woman are feeling? Write in the bubbles.

10

Picture Pack

Peasants working in the fields

Your task

1. Look at Picture Source 9. How many men are working in this picture?

2. Are they all doing the same job?

3. What jobs are they doing?

4. One of the men is the bailiff, who is in charge. Which man is he?

5. How do we know he is important?

6. What time of year do you think this is?

11

Picture Pack

The incomplete harvest

The picture below is an outline drawing of Picture Source 9. Unfortunately, parts of the picture are missing.

- There are no crops to harvest.
- There are no sickles to cut with.
- There are no staves for the bailiff to use to give his orders.

Your task

1. Complete the picture so that it looks just like the original one in Picture Source 9.

2. Here is the bailiff. What do you think he is he saying to his men? Write in the bailiff's words for him.

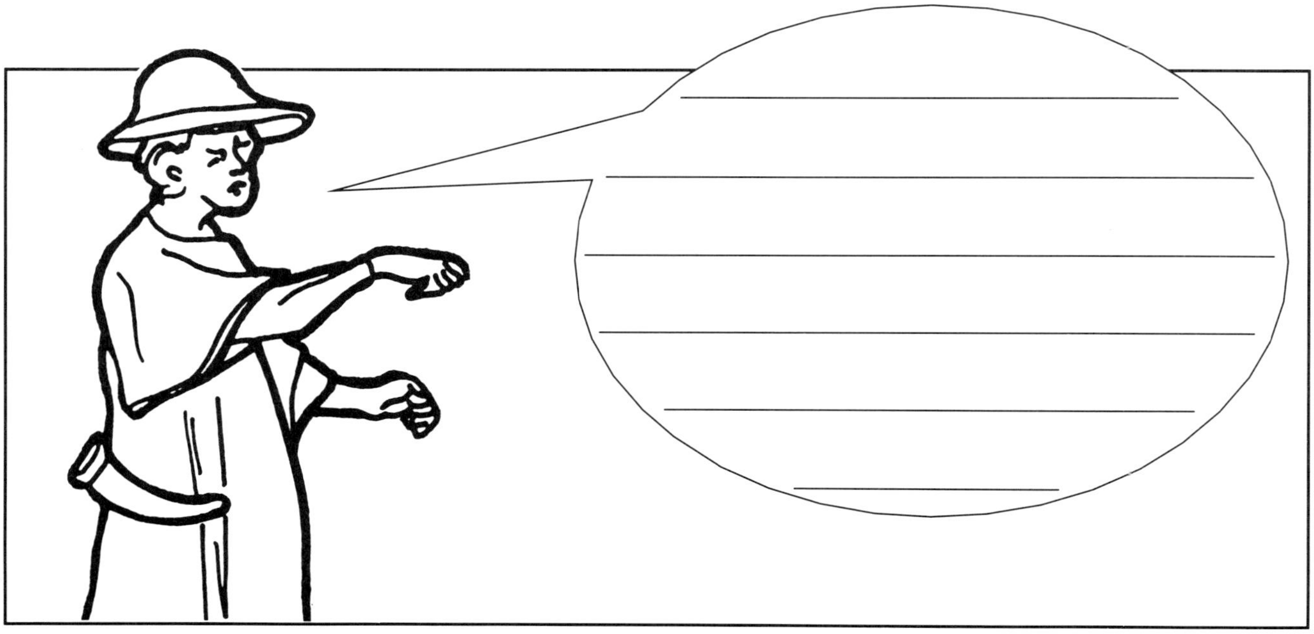

12

Picture Pack

The peasants' year

Picture Sources 6–9 were all painted by artists in the Middle Ages. The artists were showing in pictures how crops were planted, grown and harvested.

Your task

1. Copy out each of the descriptions below on to a separate piece of paper. Leave plenty of space above each one.
2. Match them with Picture Sources 6–9.
3. On a separate sheet, glue the descriptions down in the right order.
4. Above each description draw a picture to show people doing the job described. Use Picture Sources 6–9 to help you.

While the crops were growing, the peasants weeded the fields with sticks and hoes.	During the spring, the peasants sowed seeds in the fields.
When the crops were ripe, the peasants gathered them in.	The peasants ploughed the fields to get the soil ready for planting seeds.

13

Picture Pack

The harvest wagon

Your task

1. Look at Picture Source 10. What is being carried on the wagon?

____

2. Bringing in the harvest was a very dangerous job. Many peasants died or were badly injured while doing it. Mark on this drawing all the things that could go wrong. One example has been written on for you.

This man could fall and break his ankle.

14

Picture Pack

Carrying a sack of corn

Your task

1. Look carefully at Picture Source 11. What sort of building do you think is shown here?

2. How did it work?

3. Describe what you think is happening in the picture.

4. What do you think the man has got in his belt?

5. What is the dog sitting next to?

6. What are the two people thinking?

15

Picture Pack

The water mill with eel nets

Your task

1. Look at Picture Source 12. Can you find evidence in this picture that people in the Middle Ages ate bread, eels and berries? Write the evidence here:

Food	Evidence
■ bread	
■ eels	
■ berries	

2. In this picture, the artist is trying to show us how the water mill actually worked. Using the evidence from the picture, describe how you think water mills worked.

3. Look at Picture Source 11. This is also a mill for grinding corn. Compare the two mills and discuss as a class which things are similar and which things are different. Record your ideas here:

Similarities

Both mills...

Differences

The windmill...

but the water mill...

16

Picture Pack

Where will you put your mill?

The mill was one of the most important buildings in a medieval village. At the mill the peasants' grain was ground into flour. With the flour they made their bread, which was the most important part of their diet.

Below is a drawing of a village. You can also see a river, some trees and some hills.

Your task

1. You are the miller. You must decide where to build your mill. It could be a water mill or a windmill.
2. Draw the mill in the place you have chosen.
3. Explain why you have built your mill where you have.

____

____

____

17

Picture Pack

Sheep in a sheepfold

Your task

1. Look carefully at Picture Source 13. Can you find the following:
   - a man with his hands around a sheep's neck
   - a strangely shaped purse
   - a woman milking a sheep
   - a jug of milk or water
   - a bell?
2. What do you think the man is doing?

   ____

   ____
3. Why is the woman milking the sheep?

   ____

   ____
4. What sorts of things do you think the woman would have in her purse?

   ____

   ____

   ____
5. Why do you think the bell is hung on to the sheep's horns?

   ____

   ____

   ____
6. What do you think could be in the small flask on the man's arm?

   ____

   ____

We think the small keg may contain beer. Villagers drank beer rather than water. Why do you think it was safer to drink beer than water in the Middle Ages?

18

Picture Pack

'Sheepish connections'

Your task

1. Look at Picture Source 13. People kept sheep for different reasons. How many can you think of?
2. The drawings below are of objects, food and clothing from the Middle Ages. Write the name of each item above the picture.
3. Decide which items are connected with sheep, and under each one you have chosen, explain how.

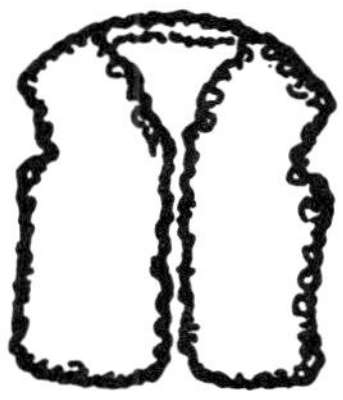

19

Picture Pack

The blacksmith's shop

Your task

1. Look at Picture Source 14 which shows a blacksmith's shop. What is each of the men doing?

2. Find each of these tools in the picture.

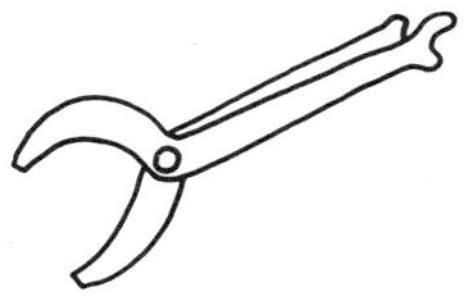

3. What do you think each tool was used for? Write your ideas below each picture.

4. Find out what each of these tools is called. Write the name in the space above each tool.

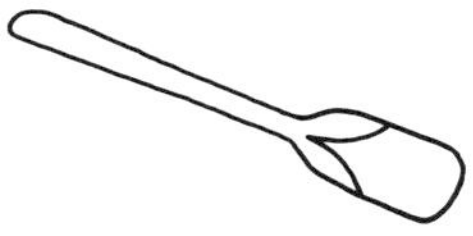

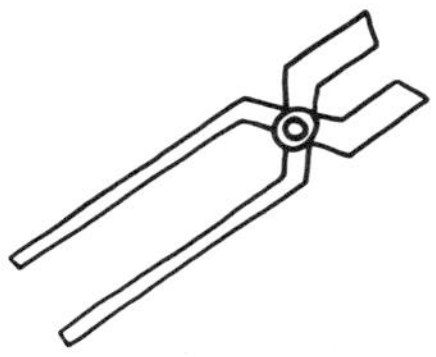

Blacksmiths still use tools like these nowadays. Why do you think the tools used by blacksmiths have hardly changed at all since the Middle Ages?

20

Picture Pack

There are two pages to this task

A medieval village scene

Picture Source 15 shows a scene in a medieval village.

Your task 1

Each of the following sentences describes something that is happening in Picture Source 15. Complete each sentence by using one of the following words:

butcher	hunting	branches	blood	baker	dough

Across

1. One woman is holding a long-handled dish to catch the pig's ________ . (5)

4. The people in the background who are riding horses are probably ________ . (7)

5. The man putting the loaves of bread into the oven is called a ________ . (5)

Down

1. The man cutting the pig's throat is probably a ________. (7)

2. The woman who is leaning over the tub is kneading ________. (5)

3. One woman is breaking ________ to put on the fire. (8)

Your task 2

Write your answers into this crossword.

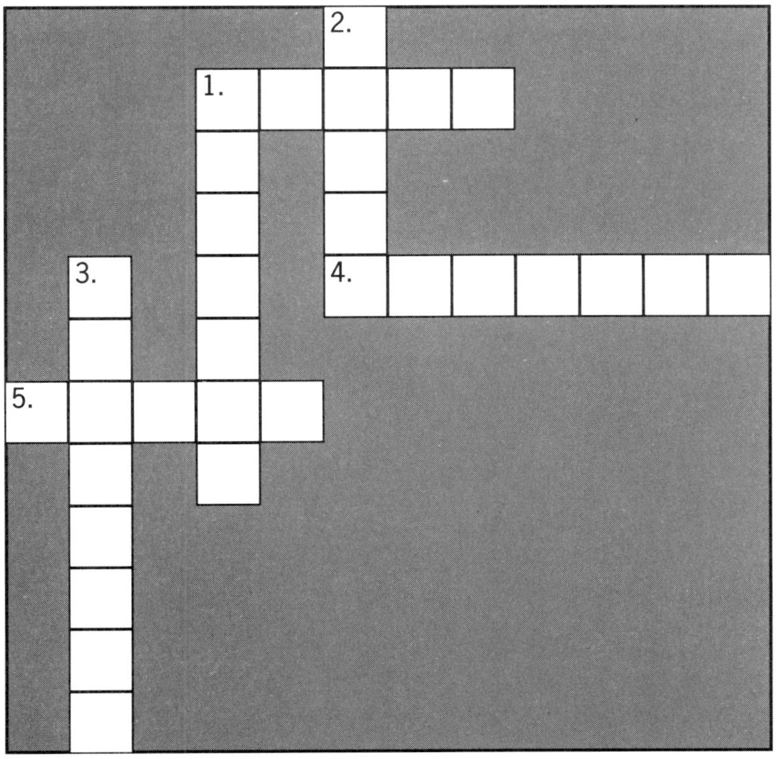

20 page 2

The activities of the villagers

Your task

1. Look at Picture Source 15. What do you think the butcher and his helper will do with the blood they have collected?

____

____

2. Why else might the woman be breaking branches? (Look carefully behind the baker.)

____

____

3. What type of building can you see between the hills?

____

4. Make a list of all the clues in this picture that tell you that the villagers are preparing for a feast.

____

____

____

5. How does this picture help you to find out about life in the Middle Ages? Tick things in the list below that you think it does tell you about. Put a cross by those things which it does not tell you about.

This picture tells me about:	✓	✗
■ the clothes that people wore		
■ the way that people travelled		
■ the food that people ate		
■ how people built their villages		
■ how people cooked and cleaned		
■ what medicines people used		
■ how people entertained themselves		

21

Picture Pack

Preparing for a feast

Your task

The picture below is an outline drawing of Picture Source 15. Write a story about the people in it. You could:

- imagine that this is a scene in a medieval village that you have studied
- give each person a medieval name
- imagine that some of the men and women in the picture are married to each other.

To get you started, you could also ask yourself some of these questions:

- Whose feast is it? Who is invited? What are the guests going to eat?
- How do the people feel (worried, excited)?
- What are they going to wear for the feast?

22

Picture Pack

There are two pages to this task

The feast

Your task

1. Look carefully at Picture Source 16 which shows a rich man called Sir Geoffrey Luttrell having dinner with his family and friends. Make a list of all the clues in the picture which tell you he was rich.

____

____

____

____

____

2. There is some cutlery on the table. What item is missing that we use nowadays?

____

3. What else can you see on the table? Make a list of items, and for each one say whether or not it would be used or eaten today.

Item	**Used/eaten today** (Yes or No)

22

page 2

What has happened to the servant?

It is difficult to work out what is happening in some parts of the picture. Can you see the servant in the middle wearing a purple robe? We think he has had an accident. We think that he has been stung by a bee.

Your task

1. What do you think has happened to the servant's hand?

____

____

____

2. In the four thought bubbles below write what each of these people might be thinking about the servant's problem.

The monk

The servant

Sir Geoffrey's wife

Sir Geoffrey

23

Picture Pack

There are two pages to this task

The kitchen in the manor house

Picture Source 17 is an artist's impression of what the kitchen looked like in a great manor house such as the one where Sir Geoffrey Luttrell lived.

You will recognise some of the equipment. It is just like the equipment we use nowadays. There are also some pieces of equipment that we no longer use.

Your task

1. Look at Picture Source 17 and use it to complete the following table.

Equipment that we use nowadays	Equipment that we no longer use
cheese grater	spit roast on an open fire

2. What is the lord of this manor going to eat for dinner tonight?

3. Is this the same kind of food that we would eat today?

Is this artist's impression of what the lord of the manor would eat as useful to a historian as the picture of Sir Geoffrey's feast (Picture Source 16)?

Spot the anachronisms: the manor-house kitchen

Your task

Examine this outline drawing of the medieval kitchen. It is similar to Picture Source 17 but some anachronisms have been drawn on it. Put a circle round all the anachronisms you can find.

24

Picture Pack

The medieval village: piecing the evidence together

You have now found out quite a lot about medieval villages through your study of different pictures from the Middle Ages.

Your task 1

Imagine you a peasant living in a medieval village. You are now going to write a description of life in your village. Some parts of the description have already been written for you. Your job is to complete it.

Copy out the description but make sure that you fill in the gaps. You can write a lot in the gaps or just a little. It is up to you.

'Life in my village' by____________________________ , a medieval peasant.

My village is called ______________________________ .

Everyone in the village has to work very hard. Some of the jobs which we have to do are ____ .

My favourite job is __________________________________ because _______________ __________________________________ .

A lot of the work we do is very dangerous. Last harvest time Agnes Bird had a terrible accident when she was helping to bring the harvest in. She __________________ ____.

In the village we keep animals such as ____ _______________________________ . These animals are used for lots of different things, such as ____ .

We eat ________________________ and drink lots of ___________________________ . We drink this instead of water because __________________________ .

Your task 2

Imagine you have to produce a display called 'Life in a medieval village' to go with your written description. The display can only consist of five pictures.

a) Choose five picture sources.
b) Write a caption for each one.
c) Explain why you have chosen each picture.

25

Picture Pack

There are two pages to this task

The town market place

Although most people in the Middle Ages lived in villages, some people did move to live in towns. The most important event in the life of a town was market day, when people could buy and sell all kinds of things.

Picture Source 18 shows a market place in a town. You can see that the buildings around the market place are made partly out of brick and partly out of wood. Above the shops and stalls you can also just see the glass windows.

Your task

1. Look at Picture Source 18 and describe the clothes that the people are wearing.

2. Look again at the village scene in Picture Source 15. How are the clothes that the peasants are wearing different from those that the townspeople are wearing in this picture?

3. What do you think the shopkeeper at the right of the picture is selling?

4. The two people in the shop on the left of the picture look as though they are making or mending clothes. Do we have people who do that for us nowadays?

5. Which of the shopkeepers do you think is a dentist and why do you think this?

Spot the anachronisms: the market place

Your task

The drawing below shows the same market place as in Picture Source 18. However, an artist has deliberately added some things to this picture which do not belong in the Middle Ages. Put circles round these anachronisms.

26

Picture Pack

Heaven and hell

In the Middle Ages most people went to church every week. They believed that if they lived a good life they would go to heaven. If they did not, they would go to hell. People were very afraid of going to hell.

Most people could not read, so to teach them about heaven and hell many churches had large paintings on the walls, like Picture Source 19. In the middle of the picture you can see people climbing a ladder. They are trying to climb out of hell and into heaven.

Your task

1. Look at Picture Source 19 and find:
   - the murderers being put into a pot of boiling water
   - a money lender being burnt
   - a bridge of spikes for dishonest tradesmen
   - a woman having her hand bitten by a dog
   - a drunken man with a wine bottle.
2. In the first box below, copy the picture of the archangel who has a pair of scales in his hands.
3. Write underneath your picture what you think he might be saying to the man being weighed on the scales.
4. Copy the picture of the devil who is holding on to the bottom of the ladder.
5. Write underneath what you think he might be saying to the people trying to climb the ladder.

The archangel	The devil

27

Picture Pack

There are two pages to this task

Noah's Ark

You probably know the story of Noah's Ark. It is from the Bible.

God told Noah that it was going to rain for forty days and forty nights. He told Noah to build a ship called an ark. When the rains began, Noah and all his family went on the Ark. Noah also put two of every kind of animal in it. When the rain caused a great flood, Noah's Ark floated. Everyone inside was safe. Everyone outside died. When the floods disappeared Noah, his family and all the animals started a new life.

In the Middle Ages, people loved stories like that of Noah's Ark. Picture Source 20 illustrates the story. The artist has included different moments in the story in the same painting.

Your task 1

Look at Picture Source 20. Can you find the following things:

- the Ark being built
- Noah organising the building
- Noah's family gathering the animals together
- God looking down on Noah
- two angels ready to protect Noah
- the floods rising
- some ships already sailing away?

Building the Ark

Noah is giving orders to all the men who are building the Ark for him. Even though the story comes from the Bible, the men are dressed in medieval clothes and they are using medieval tools.

This is useful evidence for historians. It tells us about the tools people used to build ships and houses in the Middle Ages.

Your task 2

1. Look at the outline of Picture Source 20 on the next page. Find as many tools as you can.
2. Shade in each one.
3. Try to guess or find out what each tool was used for and write your answers on a separate piece of paper.

28

Picture Pack

The Black Death

In the Middle Ages many people were killed by a plague called the 'Black Death'.

Picture Source 21 shows us how people felt about the Black Death. The skeleton on a horse in the middle of the picture is supposed to be 'death'. The skeleton has a bow and arrow in its hands. Everyone who is hit by an arrow will get the plague.

Your task

1. Look at the rich men at the top right. How are they trying to keep the plague from reaching them?

____

____

2. Why do you think the artist has shown the horse licking its lips?

____

____

3. There are bishops and kings at the bottom of the picture. How many have caught the plague?

____

4. Find the crowd of peasants. What do you think they are trying to do?

____

____

5. From the evidence in the picture, how do we know that the plague attacked everyone in society, not just the poor people?

____

____

6. 'This picture shows that people in the Middle Ages…

a) were not afraid of the Black Death'.

b) thought the Black Death was a joke'.

c) were very afraid of the Black Death'.

Choose a), b) or c) to complete the sentence. Underline your choice. Be ready to explain why you chose that one.

29

Picture Pack

The murder of Thomas Becket

Thomas Becket was the Archbishop of Canterbury. He was a very important person. He was leader of the Church in England.

Thomas Becket had an argument with King Henry II. They were very angry with each other. The King sent his knights to Canterbury Cathedral where Thomas lived. Picture Source 22 shows what the knights did when they reached the cathedral.

Your task

1. Read Source 1 which describes what the knights did.
2. Underline everything in Source 1 which is also shown in Picture Source 22.

SOURCE 1 An account of Becket's death written by William Fitzstephen, Becket's friend

One of the knights struck the Archbishop between the shoulders with the flat of his sword. He said 'Fly. You are a dead man.'

Edward Grim, one of the monks, put out his hand. He was hit by the first stroke of the sword and was badly wounded. By the same stroke the Archbishop was wounded in the head.

As the Archbishop knelt down he stretched his hands out to God. A second sword stroke hit him on the head. He fell by the altar.

While the Archbishop lay there Richard Brito struck him with such force that his sword was broken against the Archbishop's head. The saintly Archbishop received four wounds in all.

The whole of the crown of his head was lopped off. But he didn't try to avoid or stop the blows. He accepted death.

Hugh of Horsea extracted the blood and brains from the hollow of his head with the point of his sword.

30

Picture Pack

There are two pages to this task

The Peasants' Revolt

In 1381 peasants from Kent and Essex rebelled. They attacked a government tax-collector. They destroyed buildings and then they marched to London. They were tired of paying high taxes when they only just had enough money to feed their families.

Picture Source 23 shows the peasants meeting King Richard (who was only fourteen years old) at Smithfield. This picture was painted about sixty years after the revolt. In those days artists who used pictures to tell a story would often show the different parts of a story in the same picture.

On the left you can see the peasants' army. You can also see the Lord Mayor of London hitting Wat Tyler (one of the peasant leaders) with his sword. The King is watching (perhaps he is telling the Lord Mayor to stop).

On the right you can see the King riding over to the peasants' army.

Your task

Here are some statements which tell the story of what happened at Smithfield. There are some differences between the statements and the painting.

Put a tick if you think the event is also shown in the picture. Put a cross if you think it is not shown in the picture, or the picture is different.

Event	✓	✗
Wat Tyler went up to the King, dagger in hand, and spat at him		
Wat Tyler then stabbed the Mayor of London in the stomach		
Out of sight of the peasants, the Mayor of London hacked down Wat Tyler		
King Richard rode up to the peasants		
King Richard told the peasants to obey him		
The King let the peasants go home safely		

The Smithfield story

Today we would not draw different parts of a story in the same picture. We would use a cartoon strip to show the order in which different things happened.

Your task

Draw pictures in this strip to tell the story of what happened at Smithfield. Use the statements and Picture Source 23 to help you.

History Dictionary

Part 1: medieval people

archbishop
Archbishops were priests who had been put in charge of all the other priests and bishops in England. Archbishops had to obey the **King** and the Pope.

bailiff
The bailiff worked for the **lord**. He made sure that everyone farmed the lord's land properly.

the King
The King was in charge of the whole country. He was the ruler. Everyone had to obey him. The King could make all the laws. He decided when to go to war with another country. His eldest son became the next king.

knight
Knights were soldiers who fought for the **King**. They paid taxes to the King. They rented land from the King.

lord (of the manor)
The lord was in charge of the village (which was also sometimes called a manor). Most people in the village worked for him.

peasant
Peasants lived in villages. They worked in the fields for the rich barons or **lords**. They had to obey the **King**. Peasants were very poor. They had to pay **taxes** to the King, the barons, and the Church. They had to give their best corn, bread, vegetables and beer to their lord. They had to fight in the King's armies when there was a war. Peasants were sometimes called serfs, villeins, cottars or freemen.

Part 2: historical concepts and terms

anachronism An anachronism is something which does not fit in a particular period of time.

evidence Evidence is anything which we find out about the past. Historians look for evidence in historical sources.

heaven People in the Middle Ages believed that heaven was where God lived. All Christians tried to do what the priests told them so that they would go to heaven when they died.

hell People in the Middle Ages believed that hell was where the Devil lived. All Christians feared that if they did not do what the priests told them, then they would be sent to hell when they died.

medieval Medieval means 'from the Middle Ages'.

Norman A Norman is someone from Normandy in North-west France – just over the sea from southern England.

plague The plague was a terrible disease which swept through England regularly during the Middle Ages. The worst plague was the Black Death in 1348 which killed almost half the people in England.

revolt A revolt is a protest. In the Peasants' Revolt of 1381 the peasants protested against a new **tax** they were being forced to pay. Often a revolt can be very violent.

tax Tax was money people were forced to pay to the **King** or the Church.

S·H·P THE SCHOOLS HISTORY PROJECT

DISCOVERING THE PAST: MEDIEVAL REALMS PICTURE PACK WORKBOOK

Use evidence from the Middle Ages to find out for yourself:

- how William invaded England in 1066
- what life was like for ordinary people in the Middle Ages
- what kind of problems kings had in the Middle Ages

JOHN MURRAY

This workbook is based on the 23 pictures in the Medieval Realms Picture Pack (ISBN 0-7195-5382-2)

ISBN 0-7195-7056-5

9 780719 570568